CREATIVITY

Your Daily Gift

Meredith Gaston Masnata

Hardie Grant

BOOKS

CONTENTS

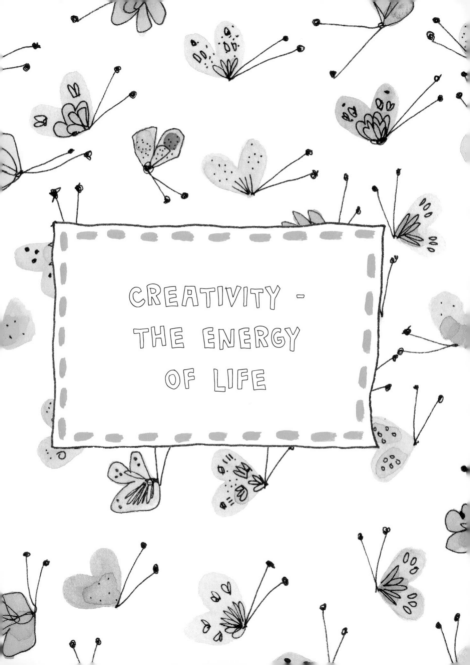

CREATIVITY -
THE ENERGY
OF LIFE

The same creative energy of life that turns
the colours of leaves in autumn, makes rain
fall and stars sparkle, makes day follow night,
rainbows span the sky and in-breaths follow
out-breaths is the very same energy and
intelligence from which we are made.

As human beings we are organically, wondrously part of our natural
world. We are ever-evolving creations in motion, moving about
a vivid, mysterious and marvellous universe of limitless creative
energy – of beginning and endings, transformation, change and
growth. In our aliveness, we are inherently and effortlessly creative.

The quality of our lives and our joy depends on our willingness to understand and embrace creativity as our energy for life, and as our very personal gift to unwrap, discover and enjoy to the fullest each day.

Just as a sculptor explores the beauty and bounds of clay from an imaginative seed in their mind, creating something from nothing, we sculpt our very own realities with our thoughts and ideas. Harnessing the infinite potential of our personal creative energy, we can all play, explore, endeavour and innovate – forever learning and growing as we live. We can all use our unique imaginations, hearts and hands to make something beautiful. Indeed, our greatest works of art will always be our very own lives.

It is both tragic yet easy to claim a lack of inspiration or ability, thereby dismissing our inherent creativity. It is harder but infinitely more rewarding to learn to open our eyes to the endless inspiration that dwells within and around us – to the lusciousness of being and the mystery of life. To do so we must awaken our senses – a life-changing art we will learn to cultivate in this small but empowering book. Living with our senses awakened, we come to find inspiration in even the littlest and simplest of things. Life becomes a joy – a blank canvas – an opportunity for self-expression – an enquiry into the richness of being – an interactive, synergistic communion with the world around us.

To disregard our creativity is to diminish our life force. To embrace our creativity is to become both luminous and illuminated in this life, elevating our energy, sense of purpose and wellbeing.

Thinking is often misunderstood and greatly underestimated as
a completely creative art, yet is the most powerful and creative art
we will ever come to know and love. Our gift of creativity takes
that which dwells in our minds – our imaginations – and makes it
manifest. With our thoughts we build worlds within and around us.
What we think, we become. What we choose to see, we see. What
we believe is possible or impossible for us becomes so. Accordingly,
the world becomes as limited, lacklustre and uninspiring – or as
limitless, alive and magical – as our imaginations make it. The
moment we understand this is the moment we recognise creativity
as our innate superpower. In the following chapter, we will dive
deeply into this vital concept, unpacking and exploring it.

Albert Einstein asserted that creativity is more important than knowledge. Indeed, our imaginations determine our personal experience of life by colouring our vision of it. From foundations built in our minds – our unique ways of seeing, thinking and feeling – we generate exciting scaffolding for our worlds as we know them. In our openness to learning and growing through life, we live fully – we are humbled, inspired and gifted. We become all that we can be, contributing to life in wonderful and meaningful ways. The generous energy of creativity, in its sweetness, then paints the icing on our proverbial cakes of life, treating us with profound delight.

We find that life is enjoyed to the fullest as a creative adventure – joyously and gratefully savoured in reverence and integrity.

We are all original, creative beings at birth. 'Creative' is not something we have to *become*, it is something we *already are*. Some of us simply lack faith in ourselves, dismiss our inherent creativity, or even stand in our own way, stifled by self-imposed limitations, judgement and perfectionism. In doing so, we deny ourselves great pleasure and fulfilment. We deprive ourselves of the opportunity to deepen into ourselves and life.

Art is not reserved for artists, nor poetry for poets, words for writers or music for musicians. We are all artists, poets, writers and musicians in our own right, and we must embrace ourselves as such if we wish to be happy.

During my time at art school I was told that I could not draw. When I was asked to draw a three-dimensional teapot in front of the class, the teacher looked at my flat, childlike form on paper and suggested I chart another course in life. I went on to study literature and philosophy instead, while making a living off my artwork – art that gave me life as I gave life to it. Art that still nourishes my spirit.

Do not be discouraged. Do not dismiss yourself as an uncreative person. The good, kind people who have attended my watercolour classes over the years and told me that they could not draw – that they did not even want to pick up a pen or paintbrush – invariably created some of the most beautiful and sincere artworks I have ever seen. I remain touched by them, and perpetually moved by the beauty, joy and power of creativity.

Plato taught that life is to be lived as play. Make this world, and your very own life, a beautiful and wondrous playground of dreams. Learn to bring your creativity to anything and everything you do. Enjoy creativity as a bedazzling gift, respecting, cultivating, sharing and treasuring it. Explore imaginative ways to enrich your daily life, to know limitless gratitude and inspiration. Turn the page now … let's go on.

AFFIRMATIONS

I am naturally crafted
from creative energy.

I am ready to experience
my gift of creativity.

Creativity is the energy
of my life.

PRAYER

As I learn to understand creativity in a whole new way now, may I sense my own innate creative energy — the vital energy of life. May my willingness to experience myself as a creative creature permeate every aspect of my life with freshness and inspiration. As I awaken to the joy of creativity in my life, I begin to cultivate respect for the person I am — for my unique imagination and ways of self-expression, my own thoughts and ideas, and my own innermost hopes and dreams. I lean into my heart now, drawing on my own personal wellspring of creative energy — energy that regenerates in infinite, sacred and effortless connection to the energy of all there is to know and love on earth.

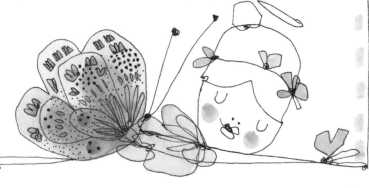

THINKING AS A CREATIVE ART

It is life-changing to understand and enjoy thinking
as a creative art. Let us begin by learning to
respect, acknowledge and work lovingly together
with our thoughts as the sculptors of our lives.

To think well is to live well. Thinking well is not a complicated art, but it is the most important art of all. It requires common sense, self-respect, and respect for the tremendous power of our minds. It requires us to embrace our innate, limitless creativity and to appreciate the gifts of life and living. By empowering ourselves with stimulating, uplifting and inspirational thoughts, we may greet each day with freshness and enthusiasm – journeying as creative beings, and truly living with intention and purpose.

While we may not realise it, each and every thought we choose to think is creativity in motion. Our thoughts determine the way we see and experience life, moment to moment. Woven together, these thoughts and moments become our unique life stories.

Thoughts are creative expressions and we are the creators of them. Each thought we choose to think is productive, shaping our personal reality and experience of life. Our thoughts dictate the way we see, feel and behave here on earth, form our beliefs and attitudes, colour our personal energy, and even determine our state of health and happiness. Our chosen thoughts can support or scare us, inspire or demotivate us, empower or diminish us. This concept is not complicated – it is very simple.

We are all creators, by virtue of being thinkers.
We are constantly creating. And, as we elevate
the quality of our thoughts, we elevate the
quality of our lives. With imagination, we can all
design and create more marvellous and energising
experiences to satiate, enrich and inspire us.

As we grow and change, weaving the tapestry of our own lives, we can inadvertently lose touch with the power and potential of thinking as a creative art. Negative, fearful and unappreciative thinking dulls our senses and degrades our vision of life.

In a version of reality coloured by a self-limiting and lacklustre world view, natural creative thoughts can be stifled, forgotten, dampened and even extinguished – like the snuffed light of a once glowing candle. As children we know that we are candles, each with our very own light to share. We unashamedly share our gifts and our love.

If we wish to nurture our glow and experience
creative, fulfilling and balanced adult lives,
we must take care of our thoughts.

Negative, limited thinking void of imagination and wonder is not
natural in our busy 'grown up' world – it is a choice. Our thoughts
are malleable, flexible and dynamic. They can be changed. And as
we change our thoughts, *we* change.

Habitually intercepting and redirecting unwanted thoughts unmasks and discharges them. It also reminds us that we are the creators of our thoughts in what is the masterpiece of our own lives. We are not our thoughts, we are the *thinkers* of them. We are the intelligence and creativity at the helm of our thoughts. In our essence we are free spirits, connected to the great spirit of life from whence we all sprung – the very wellspring of all creativity. Just a single moment acknowledging ourselves as divine, creative beings in a universe of miracles can catapult us, with appreciation and awe, into the power of the present moment – this moment. The moment in which anything and everything is possible.

With our thoughts we can create worlds of our own in which to dwell in peace and joy, living by example and lighting the way for others to explore and experience their own dream of life. Positive, uplifting thoughts create positive and uplifting experiences. Indeed, when you choose to view, live and enjoy life through a joyous lens, you see just how interesting, moving and beautiful your days become. Avail yourself of the perennial magic and mystery of life and find yourself inspired. This is creativity at thought level. This is creativity – our greatest gift and treasure – our key to bliss.

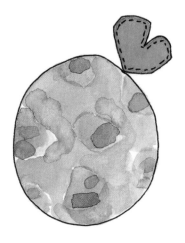

We must take control and direct our thoughts with
loving attention and intention. How tremendous
it is to acknowledge ourselves as the creative
people we truly are, and to align our thoughts,
feelings and beliefs with our innermost values and
dreams. To be inspired ... to imagine ... to create.

Even if you have chosen to think negative, disempowering thoughts
until this very moment, even if you have considered yourself
uncreative, you too can change. You can choose to think differently
now. Now is, and will always be, your only time to live.

AFFIRMATIONS

I have the power to think
elevated thoughts.

My thoughts inspire and nourish,
support and delight me.

I choose my thoughts to create
a world I love.

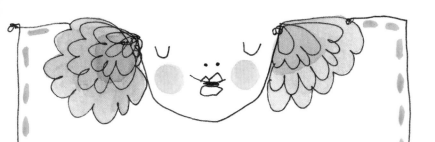

PRAYER

As I guide and embrace my thoughts, may I feel empowered. May I sculpt the life of my dreams with the thoughts I choose to think. Each time I lovingly reaffirm that happiness and peace are at home within me, I feel my strength reinvigorated. May I cultivate deeper faith in myself and life, and may my elevated thoughts become the building blocks of my exquisite personal reality.

CREATIVITY FOR
EVERYONE

Creativity is not a part of life, it is a way of life. We can bring creativity to anything and everything we do, from making our beds to baking a cake, from setting a table to singing a song. As we bring our creativity to life, life rewards us with joy and inspiration. Life is what we make it. And what we give to life, we receive in return — and in great abundance.

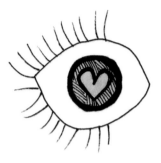

When creativity exists, boredom cannot. Creativity always sees interest, beauty and potential in things. To explore and celebrate our creativity is to assure ourselves that we will never be short of entertainment or inspiration again, nor experience deficits of delight and wonder. Creativity is for everyone, and inspiration awaits us everywhere we turn.

Many of us suffer because we consider ourselves to be uncreative. This is a self-limiting opinion that is best immediately addressed and transformed. As we have learnt, we are all creators by virtue of being thinkers, and as children, we explore our creative gifts unbridled, in manifold ways that make our hearts sing.

When we reserve creativity for those who engage with creative arts in a professional way, we truly underestimate and deprive ourselves. We forgo exquisite, nurturing and satisfying daily pleasures of all kinds, not to mention the possibility of bringing healing and harmonising balance into our days through imaginative living. The joyful play of creativity expands our minds and refreshes our spirits. Indeed, work, rest and play in thoughtful balance creates inner peace – the sense of a life well lived. We needn't miss out on anything in life when we cater to the creative needs of our spirits – to be expressive, to play and to be free.

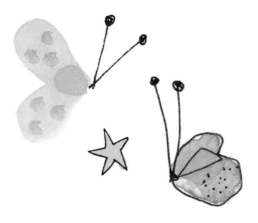

Each morning when I wake up, I greet the day with sincere gratitude. I make the bed with love. I make tea with appreciation and breakfast with care. I put things in their place and enjoy the quiet sense of calm such reverence brings. I choose my clothes with thoughtfulness and dress myself as a creative pleasure. I do my hair in the same spirit. I am present in conversations with my loved ones, listening carefully and consciously choosing my words. I write my letters and emails with creativity, adding interesting words and pictures wherever possible. I arrange flowers around the house, savour thoughtfully selected music and light candles at dinnertime, bringing a sense of occasion to each and every day. I respect other people's energy, intelligence, time and care, too, and in doing so, bring the very best of myself to life. This is not exhausting, time consuming or complicated.

This way of life is not lived with an agenda.
This is life lived for life's sake – life lived
as prayer – life lived as play.

'I don't have the time for such niceties and follies!' you may say. My reply: it takes no longer to think a positive, inspiring and beautiful thought as it does to think a negative and uninspiring thought. The difference is that a negative, tired thought will deplete your energy, motivation and inspiration while a positive, beautiful thought will invariably precede another one, and then another, and another. A creative life is built in this way – one inspired thought in front of another. When we choose to see and live life as creative beings, time expands before our minds, hearts and eyes. Indeed, life presents itself to us in a whole new way, and with the time, space, capacity and energy to live differently, we joyously discover ourselves anew.

Living creatively and embracing ourselves as creative beings in daily life makes us more interesting, unique, endearing and fresh people. Creativity softens us where we have stiffened to life and frees us where we have become rigid. Creativity expands us where we have become stuck in our ways of thinking and being, and brings the richness of colour and texture to our lives.

Bring your own unique, original flair to all that you do. Take interesting photographs. Keep a journal and jot things down by hand. Write messages with zest and wrap gifts with care. Find imaginative ways to show your appreciation, to say you are sorry, or to tell someone you love them.

A life of true excellence is a thoughtful life lived in sincerity, creativity and love. Indeed, such a life exists in a sublime space above and beyond any fussy material riches, fleeting gratification or accolades. The most satisfying, authentic and rewarding life is a life inspired and guided by the endless pleasures, great and small, of infinite creativity – in which we gift our own unique love to all things and all parts of life in a spirit of openness and gratitude. Such a life becomes a natural symphony of heart, hands and mind, joyously conducted by an unlimited imagination.

AFFIRMATIONS

My creativity is limitless and natural.

Inspiration exists all around me.

The more I welcome my creativity,
the more creative I become.

PRAYER

Awakening to the possibility of bringing my creativity to anything and everything I do, I meet life afresh. I discover within and around me a world of richness, beauty and inspiration. May I be fortified and motivated by my gratitude for life. May I sharpen my wits to notice, absorb and translate inspiration into creative expression each day. May my life become brighter, richer and all the more meaningful for my commitment to creative living in reverent harmony with life.

RECLAIMING OUR CREATIVITY

Naturalist Ralph Waldo Emerson asserted that to be oneself in a world endlessly endeavouring to make us someone else is our greatest achievement. While we may be touched and swayed by the thoughts and ideas of others, we are the only thinkers in our own minds — we are the creators of our own reality. Conscious, creative thinking and living is natural, but it requires our loving care.

We are all impacted by influences, ideologies and stressors in our modern material world – a commercial world that too often benefits from the dulling of our creative faculties. A world in which we are told that we are not enough just as we are – that we are lacking, and in need of certain things to be complete. Yet, we are always complete. We have the power to make intelligent, creative and empowering choices and, in doing so, create wonderful lives.

The world in which we now live celebrates convenience. The 'simpler' and 'smoother' our lives can become, the more time and space we should theoretically be afforded to rest and dream, cultivate rich inner worlds, and expand our innate creativity. Alas, too many people find themselves exhausted and uninspired, sectioning their creativity off as an optional part of life rather than a *way* of life.

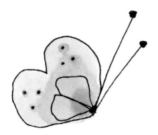

Without our wits about us, a bustling, contrasting world of separation, competition and productivity over one of peace and joy can sadden and demoralise us.

The beauty of life is lost on us when we become disengaged – operating on automatic pilot, unseeing. Disconnected from our creative power, we can become utterly oblivious to the ever-present serendipity, enchantment and abundance of real life unfolding around us.

We may find ourselves living half lives – ticking boxes, doing what is expected of us, and, at our own and others' expense, abandoning our gifts and our heart's desires. All the while, our dreams await only our own courage, faith in ourselves and in life.

Modern conveniences and modern ways of living do not always support originality, innovation and independence of spirit. It is terribly uncommercial to be happy and satisfied with oneself and one's life; to not require external entertainment, distraction or stimulation, but rather, to be able to dwell in an enriching and immersive inner world – a world of imagination from which new ideas, visions and dreams are born.

Seldom do we see people reading books anymore, using their memories over virtual search engines, calculating sums by hand or mind, savouring the joy of crafting or home cooking, or simply looking above and beyond screens to gaze at each other and the world around them. We have lost so much, and we will continue to do so until we choose to commune – consciously and completely – with our creativity. This choice will restore not only our happiness, peace and vitality but also our humanity.

Daydreaming, downtime and creative play are not idle follies. They are magical, productive and essential parts of life that cultivate greater creativity.

Jobs needn't be worked, nor projects completed or chores done as a means to an end. Rather, all endeavours and efforts can be lived and enjoyed as creative expressions of a fulsome and meaningful life. Simply touch all that you do with creativity and love. By doing so, you will find yourself more creative, nourished and inspired than ever before.

As you move through these pages, we will explore ways to do all that we do in daily life with creativity, and to channel our personal energy into building realities we truly adore. The chapter 'Awakening Our Senses', prepares us for the joy offered in the chapters 'Be Inspired: It's Time to Create' and 'Creativity in Daily Life' – brimming with inspirations, prompts and ideas for creative living.

Acknowledging that our way of thinking, seeing and being in this world is determined by our creativity, and understanding our thoughts as productive, we empower and celebrate ourselves as unique individuals. We also become naturally inspired to play a meaningful part in a greater creative collective. We feel encouraged to turn our energy to collaborative projects, experiences and moments that accentuate our happiness while contributing to the greater good, offering connection and love here on earth.

The more innovative and inspired we become
as we activate our creativity each day, the more
energised and passionate we will feel.

These satisfying feelings become our motivators, sparking more
magic in a satiating, sensational circle of life.

AFFIRMATIONS

I now embrace my natural
creative energy.

I respect my imagination and
honour my creative power.

My best life expresses and
supports my true nature.

PRAYER

May I freely express myself, allowing the truth of me to be seen and felt. May I allow myself to learn and grow with joy, experiencing life as a wondrous and welcoming playground. As I open my heart to enchantment and inspiration all around me, let me discover a whole new way of being. I ask to be graced with the insight, strength and self-respect to move beyond my self-imposed limitations now. I am ready to loosen into the magic of life and find myself softened. I am ready to embrace the fullness of my own creative potential in a wonderful world that sees my sparkle.

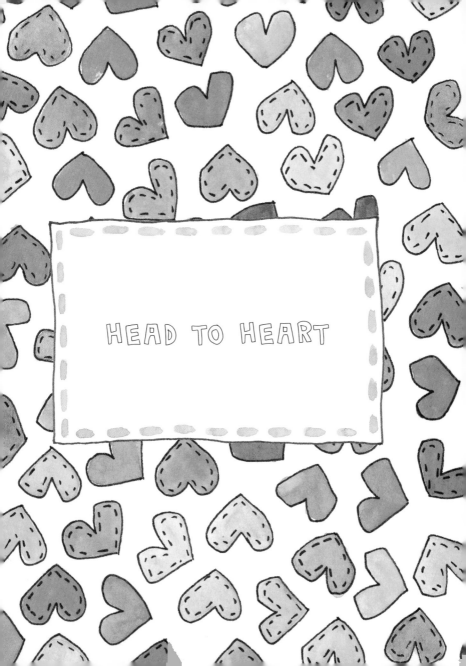

HEAD TO HEART

Expressing our creativity, especially using our
hands, can bring us down from our thinking
minds into our sensing bodies and feeling hearts.
The more time we spend in our bodies and hearts,
the more nourished, present and expansive we
feel. From a feeling place beyond analytical
thought, we can learn, enjoy and experience so
much. Indeed, as we connect with our creativity,
we connect with ourselves — igniting, satisfying,
comforting and delighting our unique spirits.

While thinking is often championed and understood as mental work, the eye of the heart is a great seer. Indeed, in ancient cultures the eye of the heart was celebrated for its unique capacity to sense and express the true essence of life – vitality, depth, purity and truth. Heaven on earth can be experienced in our hearts and as a felt experience, imbuing our minds with limitless inspiration.

As we embrace our creativity, express our individuality, imagine and create, we nurture and make manifest the seeds of our imagination, gifting new life to ourselves and the world. We must find inroads to our own heaven on earth, understanding creative flow as an ever-present portal.

We spend most of our time in the small space between our two eyes, often forgetting to inhabit the rest of our bodies and the world around us. Analysing, ruminating, living in the past or the future, stressing, worrying and overthinking depletes and tires us all.

'Growing up' at our own expense, forgetting and underestimating the pleasure, power and potential of play, makes us very serious people. Our brows furrow. Our bodies stiffen. We lack balance and feel overwhelmed by all there is to do each day. Eye contact, a genuine smile and true presence have become rare gems in our looking-down world. This needn't be so, but we ourselves must be the change.

Indeed, as we embrace our creativity, we encourage others to do the same. We become part of a more joyous, magical, softer and brighter world – a heartening place of limitless potential.

We must not 'find' the time for creative pleasure, we must 'make' the time, prioritising mindful, imaginative expression in our days.

Busying ourselves chasing happiness, status
or success in a material world can mean we find
ourselves caught up in very cerebral, dense and
uninspired personal realities. By embracing levity
in balance with respect and passion for life,
we return to our senses.

For our hearts to know joy, we must routinely interrupt our to-do lists and *shoulds*, willingly savouring time spent in creative flow. When we do this, we find ourselves so refreshed and energised that the time for all the other parts of our lives materialises effortlessly. Indeed, time is what we make it, and creativity has the power to expand time. At best, creativity imbues even our to-do lists, bringing respect, grace and delight to the littlest, simplest of things.

I take great pleasure in teaching watercolour to people of all ages, especially people for whom drawing and painting feels daunting, or like a figment of their childhood memories. As class unfolds, the room shifts from an anxious place of charged noise to a shared space of divine quietude. Thoughts slow, even time slows, as we drop down from our busy minds into our hearts and hands. Even participants who felt nervous or self-conscious about putting brush to paper invariably enchant themselves with their creations. In my eyes, any so-called 'creative block' can be remedied by descending from our busy minds into our sensing bodies and feeling hearts.

In my own home, we do not have a television. It is extraordinary how much time we find to simply *be* – to listen to music, make art, prepare and serve beautiful meals, play instruments, notice what nature is doing beyond our windows, and to be quiet and still. In the quietness and stillness of such a life, wonderful ideas may come to our hearts and minds.

When we busy ourselves too much, book
 ourselves to the brim with insufferably
demanding agendas, we do not leave any
room for imagination, spontaneity and play.
We block the magic of life from permeating
our minds and hearts, and in doing so, miss
out on the lusciousness, contentment and
meaning this magic brings to our lives.

My great grandmother's crocheted tea cosies remind me of a
time in which handcrafts were lovingly savoured, gifting delight
to makers and recipients alike. Materialised with heart, even the
humblest of our creations can generate happiness, healing and
love. By abandoning illusive notions of perfectionism that inhibit
our creativity, we can be courageously vulnerable, authentic and
generous of spirit. Respectfully inviting spaciousness for original
thought and expression, we can go forth, imagine and create.
We will be generating experiences to nourish our hearts and
enrich others with whom we share our lives. Soon we will find
that dipping down from our heads to our hearts is as natural as it
is necessary, and more delicious than words could possibly express.

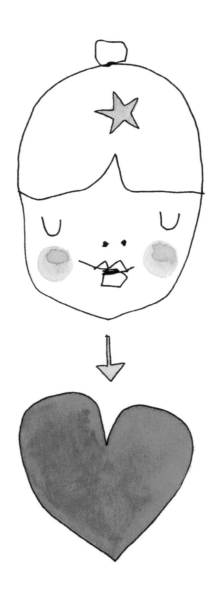

AFFIRMATIONS

My hands are alive with
creative energy.

I honour and respect the making
of things, great and small.

As I embrace my creativity,
I awaken my heart.

PRAYER

My hands hold limitless potential for infinite creation. May I honour my hands and call upon them to guide the shaping of creations, great and small. May loving energy move through my hands, imbuing all that I touch with my love. As I move down from my busy thinking mind into my feeling heart, may I come in close touch with my aliveness, emotions and dreams. May my inner world be nourished as I make the treasures of my imagination manifest. May I live a truly satisfying creative life, experiencing heaven on earth in my heart.

AWAKENING
OUR SENSES

A truly creative life blossoms with conscious
awareness of the worlds within and around us.
Our inner worlds are worlds of sensations and
feelings. They gift us our intimate, unique
experience of life as we know it. By exploring
and celebrating the richness of our inner lives
in vivid earthly context, in relationship with the
world around us, we heighten our ability to observe
and appreciate life in its infinite splendour.
Mindful living offers us all the inspiration we
could ever need to craft richly creative lives.
Let us awaken our six senses now, inviting
ourselves into a whole new way of being.

Mindful living is grateful living in the present moment. While the ability to see and feel deeply is a tremendous lifelong gift that we all possess, we can lose our connection with our true feelings and vision. In essence, what we are losing is our connection with ourselves, each other and life. When this happens, our creative energy dwindles and our happiness melts away. We simply *must* arouse our sleeping senses to fully reset ourselves. When we realise that joy and inspiration can be derived from the smallest and simplest of things, our strength grows. In honouring and exploring our lives with our senses awakened, we feel alive. Life becomes a luscious, visceral experience brimming with colour, texture and countless other sensory delights to stimulate and enrich us.

Seeing

We can miss so much when we travel through life caught up in our minds, existing on autopilot or looking down at our screens. Sadly, we constantly teleport ourselves out of our potent, precious present moment. Flowers are blossoming. Bees are buzzing. Birds are making formations in the sky. People's faces are telling stories. Secret, wonderful things are happening through windows – the world is brimming with inspiration.

'The only thing worse than being blind is having sight but no vision,' wrote Helen Keller, who herself was deaf and blind yet possessed tremendous vision for the beauty and subtlety of life. We must look around us. We must all learn to see.

Seeing things the same way makes for lazy and unappreciative eyes. Take a different route to a familiar place and notice details as you see things afresh. Move objects and artworks around in your home, move furniture and plants. Sit and observe something with care – even for just a few moments. Notice the way things are. Observe how certain things stay the same while others change. Notice how the hands of time have touched and shaped the world around you, gifting it patina and tales to tell. Soon you will find that your heart becomes actively involved in your way of seeing, and, little by little, more and more, you will find your creativity positively ignited.

Hearing

In order to awaken our sense of hearing, we must learn to listen well. As good listeners, as people sensitive to the world of sound around us, we have so much to learn, gain and enjoy. Choose new music and listen to it carefully. Choose new words to enliven and expand your vocabulary. Take notice of the intonation in your own voice and the voices of those with whom you share life. Listen for subtleties. Tune in, and you will hear so much more than the words being said. Being astute in this way can be life-changing. For instance, learning to listen carefully to our own voice and internal speech allows us to interrupt and upgrade limiting self-talk. And, as we become more savvy with this, we begin to pick up others' unhelpful language, too. In listening carefully to ourselves and others, we can become more compassionate, inspiring and supportive people.

Listen. In this quiet moment I can hear the gentle sounds of a pond, jazz in the background, a cat meowing and the muffled, distant noise of Sunday afternoon commuters. Had I not consciously tuned into the sound of this very moment, its comforting, joyous and intriguing qualities would have very likely been lost to me. Instead, this has become a moment to appreciate – to savour.

Tasting

If we wish to awaken our sense of taste, we are called to play.
If we always choose a certain menu item, we must choose another.
If we always cook a certain way, we must explore other possibilities
for culinary creation. Seek out new restaurants, explore recipe books
for inspiration or take a cooking class. Find a fun friend with whom
to play blindfolded taste-testing games or take a wine appreciation
course in a lovely vineyard. Make up your own recipes and choose
reckless abandonment and joy in the event of any failure.

Be experimental. Try very dark chocolate and let it melt on your tongue. Drink an assortment of teas and discover which ones you love the most. Try unusual fruits, vegetables and spices from the market. Grow herbs in your garden and add them to your creations. The more we embrace our creativity in the things we taste, the more confident and energised we will be, and the more delicious life will become.

Smelling

Our sense of smell may also be awakened in an inspired, creative life of endless pleasures. Think of coffee brewing or biscuits baking, lavender oil on a pillow slip or magnolias in full bloom – these are scents to delight us. There are wonderful scents to learn about and explore. Take 'petrichor' for instance – the smell of the earth after rain, or 'biblichor' – the wistful, faint and musty smell of old books. Close your eyes and savour the moment when you come upon an intoxicating, evocative scent. Let it embrace you.

Old European perfumeries were famous for personalising fragrances for their clientele, some with very specific and unusual requests: wishing to smell like freshly cut grass, sweet cinnamon, clouds, vanilla, leather or sandalwood – the list goes on. A personalised concoction would then be created.

If you could choose, what would your personalised perfume be composed of? Which scents reflect your personality, and which scents elevate you?

Essential oils offer us a world of possibilities to explore natural scents as well as offering manifold unique medicinal qualities to nurture our wellbeing. Try lavender oil to soothe your spirit or peppermint to clear a stuffy head. Enjoy frankincense for grounding or a touch of rose for sweetness and comfort. When activating your senses in a creative life, leave no proverbial stone unturned. There is so much to life – so much to enliven us and so much to enjoy.

Touching

Embrace all things with love, and love will embrace you. Be gentle in your touch – explore things. Being heavy-handed, rough, hurried or absent in the way you touch will see you miss so many chances for connection, softness, gratitude and peace. Embrace your loved ones and your pets. Run your fingers through your hair. Feel the curves of stone fruit, the softness of carpet underfoot, the cosiness of your favourite armchair. The sand between your toes, the coolness of marble. The exquisite crispness of fresh sheets or the brush of silk against your skin. Take it in.

Awakening our sense of touch gifts us with
more beautiful, sensual and stimulating lives.
Through touch, we activate our curiosity, our
passion and our appreciation for living. As we
become more aware of all our senses, welcoming
visceral experiences and pleasures of all kinds
into our lives, we naturally feel more imaginative,
inspired and connected. From imagination and
inspiration, wonderful new creative ideas
and endeavours of all kinds spring forth.

Intuiting

We may notice that our sixth sense, our intuitive sense, develops as we spend more time in an expanded state of awareness – in creative flow. We become more attuned to the magic and mystery of the universe and find ourselves a natural part of it, sensing and intuiting more than ever before. Sublime serendipity, so-called coincidences and other marvels resulting from our alignment with the energy of life start to pepper our days, inspiring us with awe and, like little lanterns, guiding our way forward. Let us smile to ourselves in such moments and give thanks. We have found ourselves in divine rhythm with life, and our world is humming and nodding along.

Notable German psychiatrist and psychotherapist Friedrich (Fritz) Perls was known for his exciting philosophy: lose your mind and come to your senses. With this, Perls emphasises the importance of self-awareness at the level of sensation in the present moment – what we can see, hear, taste, touch, smell and intuit. Our senses allow us to connect with and relate to the world around us in intimate, exquisite ways. Indeed, by 'losing our minds' in the present moment, asking our minds to step out of the way, we may, as Sufi mystic Rumi wrote, 'drink the pure nectar of this moment'. Herein lies the secret to infinite inspiration – the key to limitless creative energy.

AFFIRMATIONS

As I awaken my senses, I come alive.

I step joyously beyond thought
and into feeling.

I embrace my life with all
my senses.

PRAYER

Awaken me to the richness, fullness and beauty of life. Imbue me with gratitude so that I may be positively touched and inspired by the world around me. May I become more sensitive and attuned to the subtle world of feeling and sensing, living luscious, intimate and divine days in communion with the energy of life. Should I ever feel uninspired, return me to my senses. Help me to step beyond my thoughts and arrive fully into the present moment – this complete moment in which all the secrets of the universe and spellbinding mysteries of life are available to inspire and delight me. As I ignite all my senses, may I discover my cup of life spilling over, my heart overflowing.

We have explored the essence, importance
and value of creativity, and discovered
wonderful ways to awaken our senses to the
ever-presence of inspiration. Now it is time
to feel inspired and create.

88

The gift of individuality is something we all possess. The creative expression of our own unique spirit is the making of us. In bringing ourselves to all that we do, in seeing that small, everyday activities carried out and savoured with creativity and love are of no less meaning and significance than any grandiose project we could possibly imagine, we truly live.

There is not another you, nor another me.
There is nobody who can do things quite the
way you do, who sees the world as you do,
or who can inhabit your unique imagination.

This delightful privilege must imbue us all with motivation to create.

We must never feel as if everything has already been done, written, sung or made, that our own creativity could be insignificant or unworthy, that our creative efforts do not matter or even count. On the contrary! When we express our creative energy from a place of authenticity and sincerity, a place of gratitude, wonder and respect for ourselves and life, we can rest assured that our creations – our lives – will always be unique, meaningful and wonderful.

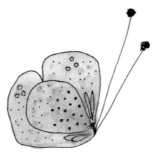

In creating lives we love and crafting whatever we wish to – a home, a painting, a playlist or a cake – we must create for creation's sake, not to win an award or others' approval, not to impress or compete, and not just for show. We must enjoy the creative journey as the reward in itself, understanding the creative process as creativity's ultimate destination.

While a great deal of focus, time, energy and even worry can be spent upon the visible results of our creative efforts, such results are the proverbial icing on the cake. At best, this icing is savoured and shared with others. We have been gifted with everything we need. We must simply come as we are, embracing our true selves with loving appreciation. We must step out of our own way and live our very own lives.

When we choose to respect the creative journey of life as our destination, we arrive into a timeless, peaceful place of belonging, expansion and meaning – a place we all by nature seek.

Life becomes liveable as an inspired adventure in full *presence* – presence both at home within ourselves, and within the vivid world around us. By empowering ourselves to live as works of art, we learn to enjoy ourselves as works in progress, constantly evolving, and shaped by our unlimited imaginations.

Our natural world is constantly generating
and regenerating all around us. We must echo
her vital energy, embracing creativity, change
and transformation within ourselves.

As we deepen our understanding, we see that chasing others' approval, accolades, or objects of fleeting desire does not make us feel the connection, peace and happiness we need. Rather, it is in the free, joyous expression of our creative energy that we feel most content, alive and whole.

In a creative life, infinite influences shape and move us. Our natural environments, patterns in the seasons and weather, the people around us, the music we choose to listen to, the colours with which we surround ourselves, the books we read and the programs we watch nourish us at a cellular level, like the food we eat.

Celebrating all the wonderful choices we have for learning, entertainment and experiences of all kinds is part of cultivating a unique, active inner life – a personal wellspring of creativity, richness and inspiration from which we can freely draw.

We are consumers of many things. It is only when we become very conscious consumers that our innate creativity may be truly ignited and elevated. By consuming less, we can create more. I, for instance, notice that I tend to read very little when I am writing a book. I look at very little art when I am creating a new body of work. At such times, I savour my existence in an intimate and completely magical world of my own – a world in which my original thoughts can float free, and from which I know I am expressing myself in my own way.

The time to embrace ourselves in a truly creative life is now. Not when we 'find' the time. Not when we finish all the chores we must do, not when we retire, go on holidays, or feel more confident in our abilities. Now is the time. Now is the only moment that truly exists, and the only moment we actually have to live. The past has gone and the future is not guaranteed. We must appreciate and enjoy ourselves as creative beings right now. In savouring our lives as perpetual creative processes in which we are the creators, we see ourselves as the original, powerful and miraculous beings we, by nature, are. Propelled by exciting thoughts, ideas and possibilities to stimulate our imaginations, we may go forth and make manifest with our hearts and hands that which we see in our mind's eye.

When we create, we literally 'realise'
our dreams, great and small.

May we dream well, freely and wholeheartedly, never holding back
when expressing our true nature and vision.

AFFIRMATIONS

Now is the time.

Creativity flows within me
and all around me.

I celebrate and nurture
my individuality.

PRAYER

I now allow creative energy to flow freely through me. I feel creative energy within me and all around me, and I warmly welcome inspiration with gratitude and joy. I honour my individuality, and I mindfully manifest the world of my dreams. When I doubt or underestimate myself, when I hold back on myself and life, support me to embrace my creativity to the fullest. May I understand the creative process itself as my destination, and find myself at home in a truly rich and wonderful life.

CREATIVITY IN
DAILY LIFE

In this exciting, hands-on chapter we will explore ways to engage our creativity daily, bringing colour, joy and freshness to our days and changing our lives as we know them. When we bring creativity to all that we do, life looks and feels different – and so do we. The word 'inspiration' derives from being 'in spirit'. Indeed, when we are inspired (which, as we have learnt, is a state of being we may actively nourish and in which we may choose to dwell perpetually), we literally invite our spirits to be delighted. We gift ourselves happiness in the truest sense. By infusing even the most seemingly simple parts of our day with our unique essence, we come to life. Let's go!

Journalling

Keeping a journal is a simple and beautiful ritual. It is therapeutic to put into words that which we think and feel. We can release our feelings onto paper, allowing the pages of our journals to bear their weight. We can lighten ourselves, inspire ourselves and watch ourselves grow, documenting our lives and honouring our days. Journalling is a personal practice – there are no rules, rights or wrongs.

While journalling in the morning upon waking, or at night upon tucking into bed can bring comfort and rhythm to our days, we can turn to our journals anytime we feel so inclined, like companions in life. Most importantly, our journals are non-judgemental spaces we create by ourselves, for ourselves, with pages upon which to express ourselves just as we are.

I recommend finding a special journal
and lovely pen to inspire your ritual.

You may wish to add drawings, colours, snippets of articles or
mementos to your pages, or you may prefer to keep them simple.
You may wish to write in full sentences, dot points, poetry or
prose … whatever comes. I keep some journals and let others go,
savouring the process of expression as my constant destination.

Writing Short Stories

How often do we create stories from thin air, generating characters, inventing scenarios, and filling a tale with colour, texture and life? Writing is not reserved for writers – storytelling is part of our human design. Be encouraged to put pen to paper or orate a story from your imagination. Be as free and creative as you can be, drawing inspiration from your dreams and the world around you. You may wish to illustrate your stories, record them in your journal, even gift them to loved ones. We all know the delight of stories, but can forget to actively participate in creating them ourselves. Enjoy your imagination and allow yourself to be surprised by what you can create. I recommend beginning with a main character – human, plant or animal. Next, give your character a personality and a sense of place. How does your character look, move, think and feel? Next, design your character a vivid adventure of learning, growing and exploration. Anything goes. If you feel stuck, break through your inertia. Let your story carry, inspire and guide you on.

Getting Dressed

It saddens me to see that many people do not care about getting dressed for the day. I savour old movies in which women wear beautifully tailored garments, silky stockings and gloves with bows, while men swan about in tweed suits, fine shoes and dapper hats. We needn't be people of great means to dress well. I personally find many treasures in second-hand stores and, to a small but decent extent, have learnt to sew myself. With love and care, getting dressed in the morning can become a creative art, an art of self-expression and a great pleasure. Select colours, shapes and textures that express your mood. Style your face and hair in a way that brings you confidence, comfort and delight. Dress first and foremost for yourself – to honour your body and your aliveness – and to honour the day. You will find your mood positively elevated. Active and lounge wear have their contexts, but truly dressing for the day has an important place too.

Choose to be expressive and original.
Cultivate a joyous, unique style of your
own beyond trend and time.

Preparing a Meal

Some come to cooking as a chore, while others cook with great passion. The point of difference is, of course, attitudinal. With a change in perspective, I have witnessed people who care very little for cooking become enamoured with this aspect of a creative life. Anything is possible. When we prepare a meal with gratitude, we imbue it with our love. It then goes on to nourish us and those with whom we share our lives and tables, as love made edible.

Choose the very best ingredients you can.
Buy locally whenever and wherever possible
and eat real foods – whole foods – connecting
you to the earth.

We are part of nature, and our bodies recognise and thrive on real, whole foods. Taking the time to cook rather than order our food is essential self-care. We must play the most important role in our own nourishment, respecting, understanding and benefiting from that which we eat. I mostly opt for very simple meals and, as a humble home cook, feel that even I can create magic for myself and my loved ones in the kitchen. Cook to music you love. Keep a clean space and use functional utensils to work comfortably with good ingredients.

Prepare all food with love, thankfulness and joy. Feel encouraged to embrace your meal preparation at a whole new level, bringing your creative energy and personal taste to this very important aspect of being alive. You will find yourself feeling nourished and flourishing.

Setting a Table

To honour a meal made with love, it is only fitting to dine at a table set with care. A bowl of fruit or a vase of flowers makes a beautiful centrepiece, with the addition of a glowing candle if you please. I do find that lighting a candle brings a sense of reverence to the dining experience, making every day feel like the occasion it truly is.

I like linen napkins and tablecloths, as they bring texture and softness to the table. I always feel as if a table is naked when undressed, and find it far more pleasant to dine at a table set with softness. A handpicked garden posy, a scattering of leaves or shells – whatever inspiring treasures you may find to bring to the table – let these become part of the ritual too, imbuing the experience with creative energy.

Tableware is very personal and a world of its own. Are you drawn to an eclectic mix of vintage plates with stories to tell, coloured glassware or cut crystal, rustic earthenware or delicate fine china? We eat with our eyes too. The way we serve our meals and the setting in which we present them become part of our nourishment. By practising mindfulness as we set the table, we curate beauty as the artists of our own lives.

With even a small amount of time and care,
we can make the ordinary extraordinary.

Making Tea

Making tea is a ritual in our household, as it is in so many cultures and households all around the world. We have a stovetop kettle that whistles for us when ready, a small collection of teapots and tea cosies, and various cups in different shapes, sizes and styles from which to drink tea. Our tea chest overflows with a symphony of flavours, from enchanting rose to energising green teas, from sleep-inducing chamomile and passionflower to calming lemon balm, soothing peppermint and warming ginger. Tea is a medicinal, healing and delightful pleasure, and the ritual of its preparation can be personalised in expressive, artistic ways that bring beauty and joy to daily life. It has been said that there are very few problems that cannot be solved over a good cup of tea. Enjoy making tea, and beatify the ritual of it to create moments of peace and bliss in any day.

Making a Bed

To my heart and eyes, an unmade bed is a vision of a morning rushed and incomplete, while a beautifully made bed is like balm for the spirit. The sight of a lovely quilt, folded sheets and pillows in place is a simple joy that can bring a sense of peace, quiet order and calm, not to mention the promise of bed's heavenly embrace at the end of the day. Making our beds with love becomes part of a cosy and comforting rhythm of life. It must be said that bed is one of my favourite places on earth. I love the peacefulness, intimacy and dreaming space it provides. I love snuggling in to drink tea, read or embrace, to journal, meditate or talk about matters of the heart.

A beautifully made bed, like a tidy home kept with love, is a sign of respect for ourselves, the spaces we inhabit and life itself. Choose colours and textures you love to adorn your bed. Let your bed become a work of art. Take those extra moments to fold your sheets, fluff your cushions and make it beautiful.

With every small, humble and sincere act of loving creativity such as this, we deepen our happiness.

Watercolouring

As my favourite medium and a long-time passion, I can vouch for the therapeutic benefits of watercolour and the joy it brings. Portable, practical, inexpensive and delightful to explore, watercolour is for everyone. In my classes, I begin with very simple exercises to loosen up and put brush, colour and ink to paper. I recommend these to you.

Prepare your creative space with a set of watercolour paints and a brush in a small glass of water by your side. Begin by simply dipping your brush in water and then into a paint colour of your choice, adding pigment to paper and exploring your colour palette. Add less or more water to your brush to create effects of opacity and transparency respectively.

See the many shades and effects you can create with just one colour. You may wish to move on to mixing colours, discovering limitless shades and tones. In doing this not only will you be exploring your colour palette, but your materials and natural techniques too. Enjoy this process, making marks on paper. This is just for you.

Graduate to simple forms on paper – flowers, stars, butterflies, or any shapes of your choosing. Enjoy creating in colour alone or introduce waterfast ink markers to embellish your coloured forms with outlines or finer details. I oscillate between starting artworks with ink and starting with watercolour, to create different effects on the page and let myself feel playful.

I recommend closing your eyes to work in ink and watercolour. This may sound odd, but try this. Take an object – in this case I will suggest a flower – and hold it in your hands. Observe it carefully. Take it in. Now close your eyes and translate it onto paper. Draw from your heart and your mind's eye. Use ink, watercolour or both for this exercise. The only rule – don't peek. Make it as simple or as detailed as you wish. When you are done, open your eyes. What do you see?

Next, take the flower in your hand and observe it carefully. Put ink and brush to paper, this time with your eyes open. Take as much time as you please. When you are ready, sit back and compare the two artworks you have created. What do you see? In most of my classes, people have bedazzled themselves by much preferring the piece they created with their eyes closed. This is a case for loosening up, creating for creation's sake, and savouring the creative process as the artistic destination.

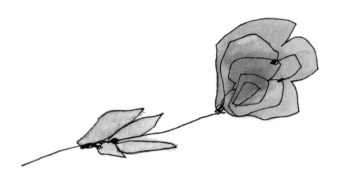

We soon learn that it is not about what it 'looks' like, but rather, what it 'feels' like.

Take your time with these exercises, allowing them to delight you. I share just a couple of simple ideas here but I encourage you to explore more. Watercolours and watercolour papers are available in art supply stores. Watercolours can be purchased in little sets, some of which include brushes. They can also be found in tubes or trays, and you can select your very own palette, growing and changing your collection over time.

Watercolours last a very long time, as only a small amount of pigment is required. I have some colours in my set from travels savoured years ago. If your watercolour set does not include a brush, ask for assistance in sourcing a brush or brushes fit for this purpose. Watercolour brushes vary in size and shape, some with rounded tips, some square, some wide, some narrow and some absolutely tiny! Watercolour paper is heavier than cartridge paper and, as you can imagine, comes in varied sizes, shapes, textures and tones too. Such paper is ideal, and important, for watercolour art, as it has the propensity to handle and embrace the water involved. Choose the nicest materials you possibly can, starting whenever and wherever you can. Enjoy this journey … what a treat it is.

Creating a Personalised Perfume

As we explored sensory pleasures in the 'Awakening Our Senses' chapter, we touched on personalised perfumes. Why not create your own using a blend of pure essential oils in a carrier oil of your choosing, such as sweet almond or jojoba oil? Essential oils are stimulating, healing, calming and enchanting. An array of citrus, floral and earthy scents awaits your discretion and personal touch. Source a little glass bottle with a dropper-style lid. Infuse a carrier oil with drops of your chosen essential oils in ratios that appeal to you sensorially, then shake gently. Add a label, if you please, creating one of your own design to embellish your creation and detail your blend for reference.

Give your perfume a name. Notice how your scent makes you feel. Might you wish to make any changes to it, adding a little more of this or that?

Experiment and explore

And don't stop at just one blend! Source a range of pure essential oils to make scents for morning and night, and generate sensations to support and delight you throughout your day. Please note that while many essential oils (blended into a carrier oil) are safe to use on our skin, some may cause irritation. We all differ in our sensitivity, too. A little research as you make your essential oil selections, along with patch testing on your own skin for suitability, is vital. This is a whole new world of creative pleasure. Breathe it in.

Curating a Playlist

Music is evocative, transformative, healing and energising, and music is for everyone. Music works on us at a cellular level, changing the way we feel. Choosing music to meet or elevate our mood is a daily creative pleasure not to be underestimated, nor taken for granted. Make playlists that inspire you, and as creative expressions to savour and share. What music helps you wake up joyfully or begin your day peacefully? What kind of music helps you focus while you are working, or brings you pleasure while you are cooking? What music relaxes you as you move about your home, or inspires you as you explore the world around you? What music do you like to drive to, stretch to or even sleep to? Awaken your senses with music and you will be creating a unique, personalised soundtrack to the art, in both stillness and motion, that is your very own life.

Crafting a Scrapbook

Scrapbooking is a therapeutic, delightful and positively addictive pastime. As we gather together pictures, patterns, textures, words and motifs that inspire our joy, pique our curiosity and express our heart's desires, we build our own visual language. In creative, tactile ways, like bowerbirds, we gather little bits of this and that to create something uniquely beautiful and uniquely ours.

With our scrapbooks, we can document our travels or special occasions, even visualise our dreams as we bring them to life. Indeed, our scrapbooks can become inspirational vision boards in portable form.

Simply begin by seeking out a blank book, ideally without lines, in which you will feel free to create. A multipurpose artist's journal, ideally with a hardcover for durability and longevity, is ideal for this purpose. Now gather mixed media elements to embellish your pages, be they coloured, patterned papers or snippets of textiles such as quilting fabrics, ribbons, lace, postcards, wrapping paper, stickers or stamps. Cut out words and pictures of your choosing from lovely magazines to bring your pages to life.

The unending joy of becoming scrapbookers is that we seek
and find so many beautiful elements with which to create,
re-emphasising the ever-present and ever-evolving delight of
creativity in our daily lives. It seems that we cannot help but gather
together quotes or ideas that resonate with us, bringing them to
our scrapbooks for joy, comfort, contemplation and inspiration.
Adding our own handwriting, sketches, even little watercolours
if the journal paper allows, makes our scrapbooks all the more
magical and personal – truly original works of art to treasure.

Creating a Home Blessing

Whether we live alone or with our pets, family or friends, the energy of our homes is determined by our attitude, our gratitude and our reverence for life. At best, our homes are sacred spaces in which we restore and rejuvenate ourselves for peaceful, joyous living. Setting an intention for our home anchors us and those with whom we share life, inspiring collective appreciation for the values upon which we build our lives and dreams each day. Blessing our homes with conscious intentions for harmony, unity, mutual respect, creativity, peace and kindness, for instance, instils a sense of direction within us – a moral compass for guidance, and a set of uncomplicated, foundational and life-affirming values to which we can return at any moment. These special values are uniquely personal – ours to determine for our own homes. Creating a home blessing is a simple but profound creative activity for everyone to enjoy. Begin by reflecting upon your values to set your intention.

Put these values into words to be displayed in a prominent position in your home. This might be in the kitchen, to be seen and enjoyed daily, or near the front door, to be read like a mantra or prayer upon arrival and departure from your sanctuary. Make your home blessing as beautiful as possible, decorated with artwork, either of your own creation or using foraged decorative elements in collage form, and then frame it with style.

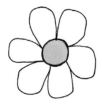

Creating a home blessing is an activity that can be savoured alone or, when home life is shared, enjoyed together. It is a creation of love and care that becomes a demonstrative commitment to nurturing nourishing, mindful lives, ever guided and inspired by our values.

Writing a Love Letter

Love letters needn't be reserved for romantic love. We can all pen exquisite, thoughtful, tender and beautiful letters as expressions of our gratitude and admiration for anyone special with whom we share life. One of the greatest regrets people harbour at the end of their days is not having adequately demonstrated and celebrated their love for others, and for life itself.

We mustn't withhold our love and gratitude. Rather, we must feel it, bring it to life and express it. We mustn't be presumptuous, assuming that others know just how we feel. We mustn't be unappreciative, taking the love in our lives for granted. We must write love letters. We must let people know how much we notice and appreciate them. Share with them their best qualities. Detail the things they do that we love, and let them know how much they mean to us. Such letters are true treasures.

You might compose a spontaneous, spirited love letter of just a few words on a little scrap of paper. Alternatively, you may take great pleasure in beautifying an expression of your love in words and pictures for your recipient. Most importantly, do not delay. As Ralph Waldo Emerson wrote, 'You cannot do a kindness too soon, for you never know how soon it will be too late.' We may never know just how much our loving words and gestures will mean to others. Write a love letter today.

This bright and beautiful list of inspirations is just the beginning. Embrace your individuality and explore your very own interests and passions as you cultivate a truly enriching creative daily life.

CREATIVITY FOR
OUR WELLBEING
AND WORLD

Choosing to embrace our creativity is a gift not only to ourselves, but an offering for a meaningful contribution to our world – a magical world in which love is the energy of life. When we bring love to all that we do, living with care, imagination and generosity of spirit, we embody the healing, fortifying and energising power of creativity. We understand and celebrate our very own propensity to spread joy and inspiration on earth, naturally becoming part of a more connected world.

In creative harmony with ourselves, others and life, we can do so much. Let us put our minds and hearts together now to explore collaboration, creative flow and the making of heaven on earth.

Nurturing our personal wellbeing by honouring our creativity in daily life makes us happier, healthier people. With the joy and stimulation of play and experimentation, the reward of projects endeavoured and shared, and the satisfaction of expressing our true selves in all manner of ways, we become brighter, more balanced and inspired individuals, able to contribute positively to life on earth. We can contribute within our immediate circles of family and friends, in our communities, and at as grand a level as we please. We are limited only by our imaginations.

In our busy world, a world in which we see and know great pain and suffering in hand with unspeakable joy, we must lean into our collective need for peace and play. One of the greatest and most beautiful aspects of exploring our creativity is entering into 'flow' state.

In flow state, time feels timeless, thoughts melt into feelings and our imaginations are unbridled.

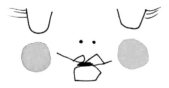

This sublime, expanded state of awareness may be entered in creative motion – playing the piano, singing a song, painting, dancing or writing poetry. Indeed, the possibilities for entering flow are endless. In my eyes, the common thread is that flow is a heavenly state. Like prayer or meditation, creative flow is a revitalising, life-affirming and positively reinvigorating communion with the great energy of life. Imagine the nourishment that could be provided to our collective spirit if each of us were to prioritise and savour time spent in this creative state. A tremendous and much-needed sense of sacredness, freedom and peace would soften, inspire and enchant our world.

As we face collective concerns together on a global scale – even as we navigate daily life – it is important for us to see that together we can do so much. Creative collaboration allows endless opportunities to celebrate each other's strengths and passions, interests and gifts. In sharing and imagining together, building and dreaming together, we find satisfaction, harmony and inspiration.

May we find thoughtful ways to connect in our families, friendship circles, schools, workplaces and communities, sharing life with respect for our immense creativity and the creativity of others. The joy we feel in making magic or generating change together has the power to move us, like a choir in divine harmony, or a flock of birds in sacred, symmetrical formation.

We can all feel world weary, tired or uninspired at times. For whatever reason, we can lose our faith in ourselves and life. At such times, it is no wonder we feel demotivated or disconnected from our creative energy. We know that we *could* do countless things, but lack the vitality to begin. Interestingly, inaction and stagnation make us all very weary. The less we do, the less we wish to do. Creative energy, like a fire, must be stoked. This stoking can be in the smallest and simplest of ways. We can renew ourselves by reading one page of a book. Savouring one flower. Taking one walk. Listening to one piece of music we love. Talking to a friend with whom we can speak from the heart. Connecting with nature on an expedition of our choosing, big or small. In my eyes, so called 'creative blocks' are simply feelings of separation from ourselves, each other and life. Wherever we go, there we are.

By taking time to know and love our unique selves, we can find ourselves at home wherever we are – at home and at peace. Embracing our creativity in daily life is an act of perpetual self-care that naturally heals, re-energises, comforts and sustains us.

With so many distractions and endless entertainment available, it is easy to become passive consumers of others' creative output. To live fully, however – to feel happy and whole – we must become active creators ourselves. We must be original in our thought and expression. We must learn to entertain ourselves, attempt new ventures, discover and savour things we feel passionate about, and participate in activities that awaken and delight our hearts. In our creative efforts we must always prioritise pleasure and progress, not perfection. We must feel motivated by the inherent reward of the creative process itself, knowing that with every loving, benevolent, creative expression of our unique natures, we are contributing to creating heaven on earth.

AFFIRMATIONS

My creativity is powered
by the energy of love.

I thrive in meaningful
collaboration with others.

I am contributing to creating
heaven on earth.

PRAYER

I am ready to share my creative energy,
to revitalise my wellbeing and invite joyous
connections into my world. I thrive in creative
collaboration and in the love, care and inspiration
of others with whom I share my life and dreams.
I choose to honour my strengths and gifts now,
and I recognise others' creative energy with
appreciation. I savour life in harmony with myself,
others and the world around me, nourished
by infinite creative energy. In daily life, in
acts great and small, I now choose to see and
create opportunities for joy, peace, healing
and connection.

DEAREST YOU,

On this continuing journey into creativity upon which
we have embarked together, I wish you the delight
of perpetual inspiration. I wish you vision to see the
meaning and beauty in daily things great and small,
and heartfelt gratitude to appreciate the infinite
pleasures and mysteries of life.

May you feel encouraged to embrace your life as
a unique adventure of your own creation. May you
honour your originality, sensitivity and true essence
in imaginative, expressive ways that elevate your spirit.
May you always make time for play, bringing balance,
joy and levity to life.

As you nurture yourself and others with whom you share your world in creative ways, and as you bring new ideas to life with your heart and hands, may you experience love, satisfaction and a sense of connection to motivate and sustain you. Feeling forever part of a great circle of life – of infinite creative energy from whence you came and to which you belong – may you activate your limitless imagination on a tremendous, awe-inspiring and unique journey of love and learning.

I'll see you there.

Meredith x

ACKNOWLEDGEMENTS

I am deeply thankful for my rich inner life and the constant, sacred connection I feel to the spirit of all things. I acknowledge the infinite blessings in my world, most importantly the love I feel and the vividness of my imagination.

I thank my family and friends for their support of my creativity, and my community of readers, each with a vision to cultivate a life better lived – a joyous, inspired life, honoured and savoured.

I express heartfelt gratitude for my exquisite husband, Roberto Masnata, who carefully read this manuscript, shared my passion for it conceptually and gently assisted with its editing. His own remarkable creativity and feeling way of being in this world gifts me with daily inspiration.

To the dedicated team at Hardie Grant who made this book possible, most especially Sandy Grant, Pam Brewster, Antonietta Melideo and Todd Rechner, I give thanks. For editor Vanessa Lanaway, designer Celia Mance and Mick Smith & co. at Splitting Image, I express my sincere appreciation.

I treasure belonging in a world of book making – a creative, collaborative and expansive world – a world brimming with magic, beauty, and the joyous promise of endless learning and inspiration.

Meredith

Published in 2023 by Hardie Grant Books, an imprint of Hardie Grant Publishing

Hardie Grant Books (Melbourne)
Wurundjeri Country
Building 1, 658 Church Street
Richmond, Victoria 3121

Hardie Grant Books (London)
5th & 6th Floors
52-54 Southwark Street
London SE1 1UN

hardiegrant.com/books

Hardie Grant acknowledges the Traditional Owners of the Country on which we work, the Wurundjeri People of the Kulin Nation and the Gadigal People of the Eora Nation, and recognises their continuing connection to the land, waters and culture. We pay our respects to their Elders past and present.

A catalogue record for this
book is available from the
National Library of Australia

Creativity
ISBN 978 1 74379 915 4

10 9 8 7 6 5 4 3 2 1

Publisher: Pam Brewster
Managing Editor: Loran McDougall
Project Editor: Antonietta Melideo
Editor: Vanessa Lanaway
Design Manager: Kristin Thomas
Designer: Celia Mance
Production Manager: Todd Rechner

Colour reproduction by Splitting Image Colour Studio
Printed in China by Leo Paper Products LTD.

The paper this book is printed on is from FSC®-certified forests and other sources. FSC® promotes environmentally responsible, socially beneficial and economically viable management of the world's forests.